Movable Islands

Movable Islands

Poems by Debora Greger

Princeton University Press, Princeton, New Jersey

Publication of this book has been aided by a grant from the
Paul Mellon Fund of Princeton University Press
This book has been composed in Linotype Janson

ACKNOWLEDGMENTS

The American Poetry Review: "Natural Forces," "Sea Change"
The Antioch Review: "Any Story," "Companion to Ships and the Sea," "Fall," "Myopia"
The Christian Science Monitor: "The Light Passages"
Crazyhorse: "The Coloring of Experience," "Grisaille," "A Second or Third Dimension"
Inquiry: "Depth of Field," "The Palace at 4 A.M."
Ironwood: "Long-Distance Swimming"
The Massachusetts Review: "Crossing the Plains," "Going to Sleep," "The First Movement," "To Make You Well"
The Nation: "Body of Work," "Calibrations," "Closing," "From This Angle," "Not You," "Patches of Sky"
New Letters: "The Painter's Model"
The New Yorker: "After Iceland, William Morris Dreams of Panama," "The Armorer's Daughter," "The Man on the Bed," "Pentimento"
The North American Review: "The Invention of Routine"
The Ohio Review: "Letter to My Sister," "White Fields"
Ploughshares: "Sleeping Beauty"
Seneca Review: "Bad Debts," "Bearings," "Fictions," "Hard Water," "Knowing," "The Life of the Remittance Man," "What Dances"
Some of the poems in this volume have also appeared in *Cartography*, a limited edition published by Penumbra Press, Lisbon, Iowa.

I want to thank the National Endowment for the Arts and the Fine Arts Work Center for their grants, and Yaddo, the MacDowell Colony, and the Millay Colony for the Arts for their hospitality.

for William Logan

On its wooded crest stood a row of low-built villas with flat-tiled roofs. Their sloping gardens were separated by new walls and iron railings; there were lawns, greenhouses, and pots of geraniums, neatly spaced along terraces with balustrades to lean on. Many of those on board, attracted by the sight of those peaceful dwellings, felt a longing to possess one, and spend the rest of their lives here, with a good billiard table, a rowing boat, a wife, or some other dream of bliss.

—Flaubert, A Sentimental Education

Contents

III

I

I wish I were the night that I might look on you with many eyes.

—Plato

The First Movement

And when a little more time has passed, two or three hundred
years, . . . everything we do now will seem clumsy, and
difficult, and terribly uncomfortable and strange.
—Vershinin, in *Three Sisters*

Next door the clock starts over by itself,
grinding its gears like salt.
A letter is undelivered. In the desert
a sentry snaps awake in a night so black
he thinks his eyes no longer open,
and he feels for the iceberg
he had been sleeping on.
Slipping. The earth
curves sharply beneath him.
There is the fall he sees
the moment before it happens
that never happens.

Another morning, the whole island
tilts into the sun.
Over the next hill
an orchestra warms up.
The constant "A." The first movement,
andante cantabile.
He leans in the doorway,
half in or out,
and lifts his hand in a wave
although no one else is in sight.

The Armorer's Daughter

My father is a hard man.
When my mother couldn't give him a son,
he made the best of it, that is
he made me into what was missing.
So I polish a breastplate until
my smudged face is reflected blue-black
and my arm is stiff as a gauntlet.

I have my father's stubborn jaw
they tell me, those boys from the village
who tease, envious of my lot.
The roughened men who come for a mending,
who bring their smooth sons to be measured,
say I have his hands, too wide for a woman.
Then I think of the beetle on the stoop
whose shell shamed the finest armor.
It scuttled away when I reached down.
With his hand.
                    I am and am not him.
Give me the dusty wings of the moths
that dared spend the night on his workbench
and I would fly—where?
Out to the hill with the shepherd?
To the mill where the miller's son
is clouded in the finest-ground flour?

This wool-gathering angers my father.
he pounds music from metal,
a chorus of glow and chill, bend and stay.
I drop a helmet with a carelessness
I barely recognize and run into the yard,
into the road, tripping on my skirts.
Late afternoon, after a rain, already
the sun's low flame lights the edges
of everything. This world shines,
rings and shines, like his dream of heaven.

Painted Desert

Another day knocking in the orchard—
a long-necked machine shaking almond trees
branch by branch, making the sound of someone
hitting the door, demanding entry.

But when I go to answer it, the door gives
under my hand onto a wall of heat.
Crawling out of leaves, a truck rattles to the road
just ahead of its dusty shadow.

What is hospitable about this parched landscape?
Colors present themselves as limply as waxes
left in the sun: plain brown, a little green,
a poor gold, blue that glares.

When have I not thought in these shades?
The poverty of imagination, taking what is given
as simply given. The pink Englishman,
on his antediluvian bike, wears pale,

buttoned-up layers of clothes as armor
against the weather. On what used to be
a kitchen chair in what was a garden,
his brown daughter shakes her straw-blonde hair

down across her shiny shoulders. She's winding
white yarn. Why do I detail, at such length?
It's like this that I love you, like dirt
which lies everywhere like water after long rain.

The Coloring of Experience

Against the tinny sky, scattered
on the elm's blackened branches,
the pale half-coins of its leaves
seemed a kind of wealth to the kid waiting
in the remnants of a rain for some adult
to finish with another.

I could say that while she stood squinting
in the refractable air, up in the house
a woman was suggesting to the girl's short father
that in bed everyone's the same height.
Or was using some similar line to maneuver him
down the hall. But no such grown-up

knowledge is tied to that tree,
that flat light. Just this: what I saw
when I was eight was someone else's vision
and unreportable. Still. Now I wonder
what those two middle-aged, middle-class
American tourists thought when

at Versailles both separately saw
an eighteenth-century courtier
cross a bridge no longer on the map.
Though companions, they didn't
speak of the outing for years and, when
they did, only to a third person.

Letter to My Sister

Today there is only a man and a half, and it is as still
as the desert. . . .

—Masha, in *Three Sisters*

On the way home I stopped
and listened to the ice
cracking in straight lines south,
lines the wild geese take.
The day turned from the sun
toward the cold that is the home of everything.

Tonight, tired of this house, this skin,
I think of the weight of darkness
on your house at the edge of the desert.
You in the old rocker, not rocking,
listening—to what?
"Wolves in the winter," your letter tells me,
"One never sees them.
How is one to sleep without them?"

One late afternoon
the wind filled your hair like a flag,
and your words blew against your face.
You crushed a sprig of sage
until the air was full of the smell,
half medicinal, half wild.
I remember that but nothing with it.
What am I looking for? Something small.
A twig to take me back. A twig to send me on.

Depth of Field

The last of the light rusts around us.
On your chest, a book's pages
ruffle in your slow breath.
Your camera, accurate about your children's
reluctance to stand still,
would freeze this flutter and miss
the one inside, your heart's
uneven, stubborn rhythm.

The book's about a tribe whose men,
on a long hunt, hollow little depressions
in the plains and sleep there,
to wake at dawn under a sheet of frost.
It doesn't say how the man
who discovered them spent his nights.
Or what drug is making you sleepy.

There's a photo in which one of us,
crying, has run from the pose
—to be captured, blurred fist
to bleary eye, in the corner of the frame.
You didn't know your own strength
the way we did, hugged hurriedly
after a sitting, in a tangle of cords and lights.
You don't know what remains of it.

Monet, in his last, huge, hazy paintings,
depicted water lilies, details
that for another painter would have been
just background. Middle distance,
depth of field—with sky-shaded eyes
you've been scanning what's out there
but listening for something else,
somewhere inside.

Pentimento

Old paint on canvas, as it ages, sometimes becomes transparent.
When that happens it is possible, in some pictures, to see the
original lines: a tree will show through a woman's dress, a
child makes way for a dog, a large boat is no longer on an
open sea.

—Lillian Hellman

Across the meadow a change of cloud comes
and, looking up, you see what you can't hear,
a whiteness falling, filling the cracks
in the old scenery, icing the aviary
and the stuffed bird on a summer hat.
Someone wearing white gloves
plays the white keys of a piano,
unaware that she is overheard. Caution,
that crumpled handkerchief,
is thrown to what wind there is.
The white creatures begin to appear:

The floury hands of your mother.
The clouds of her breath around your name.
The white shoes of summer.
The white arms of the tree you loved
and fell from. The white hair
of a girl you covered with leaves
under that tree. The white breast
hidden in the white dress.

A varying hare ventures into this
softened landscape, feeling safe
from the snowy owl. This is its error.
Yours is of a different order.
These things you had forgotten
have nothing to tell you.
You open the door to see more clearly.
There is the field, green,
and dark birds breaking into flight.

The Light Passages

A day later than he said in the letter,
still humming, half-whistling
the theme of the piece he stayed on to practice,
he leaves the car at the last road sign
and climbs the fence, taking the old shortcut
through the orchard at sunrise.
He stumbles through weeds,
sending up sleepy birds,
the only sounds their stiff wings
and ice cracking on the branches
from which they have risen,

thinking not of them but of how
Beethoven, playing a new sonata for friends,
hardly touched the keys
in the *pianissimo*,
imagining a light passage
that the others, not deaf, could not hear.

From the porch he looks back—
the orchard, still again,
is another world, a trick of the eye,
as the house in silhouette was before.
The house, still dark inside,
is still home.
Careful not to wake his family
after all the years,
he slips through the door
and surefooted as if he had never left
goes to the piano
and begins to play.

Physical Properties

After three days of wind
compounding itself, early this morning
it knocks the power out. What hour

was it last time? Prime, and your brother,
a groggy acolyte, extinguished a candle
he'd just lit, daydreaming of more sleep.

In the poor light of that hour,
a schoolgirl—you—discovered she was
wearing one black sock, one blue,

as she fumbled for the romantic novel
buried in her bookbag. Another
winter circus, these slippages

of memory, this hold. Like an acrobat
hurtling from her horse toward the paper-
covered hoop, you feel in the dim chill

you're moving into the embrace of a man
unaware of his size and attendant strength.
Maybe, like velocity, the fear is made

as much of duration as of direction.
That girl trying not to devour her story.
What the book didn't cover—

all properties of inertia. Maybe
it's just a matter of articulation.
Iced oak leaf stubbornly shivering

on its branch. This man's elegant jointing
braced to break your fall. These words,
involuntary as breath: *This is what I*

want. This hour is what I want.

13

Bad Debts

You peel an orange for someone
who's again bitten her nails to the quick.
She ignores the gesture's fruit,

but who can miss the sharp oils released?
The air is as freighted as that
over mint fields during harvest,

something shot past, caught afterwards.
The civil voices of your parents
wafted away as you drowsed in the back seat.

Beside you lay the shell, lime-whorled,
ripe with death's salt and stink.
Against your ear, its waves matched

the waves of your blood, giving back
what you are always left, that thief
of the moment, yourself. You owe something

still to that shell just as this woman
must owe you for wandering when you did
and for coming back as if to some other room.

She offers you an orange segment
but lets you open her hand and follow
the almost moonless nails, their calendar

of tenses, because it has nothing
to do with her. It's yourself you must
pay back, blankness for blankness,

kindness in kind.

From This Angle

You look older, pearled, captive
of light that outlines like ice
sheathing a tree. Ruthlessly delicate,
it edges you like snow settling on a twig,
crystal by crystal.

Though this is not the city
he never left, Vermeer would recognize
the light and you holding a letter to it,
a patch of sun pushing your hairline back.
For two hours on a good day the light was his
to arrange certain things in: map, heavy
blue chairs, clay jug and, implied beyond this,
the leaded window, the challenge of the familiar.

For two hours we've heard trees
breaking their clear shells, scattering shards
on the crusted snow. Across the street
an old woman beats a sapling with a broom.
You refold the letter in your precise way
and we laugh, as if it were funny,
about what my mother forgets she's told us.
You rub your face as if rehearsing age.

Body of Work

Counting under her breath, intent
on landing in her partner's arms,
on making it look as natural
as the collision at an intersection

of two strangers unaware that they share
a lover, the dancer can't tell you
what music she crosses to: Something
with a beat. Her own pulse?

Something for violin and piano.
What Beethoven wrote for a man who found it
impossible. What Tolstoy used
to drive a character to murder.

Something left spinning because
to stop, to rise before you, to cross
the long room and not to break anything
is beyond me. Encased in this body,

I see to the end of the street, not far
enough to see the rise of mountain,
the scar where, under sky of a season
out of place, lightning clawed its way down.

I feel the charred face brood, as I do.
How I hate this body, its stupid,
sullen secrets. Its armed resistance
in the face of—I can't say it.

A disease. Incommunicable. Stubborn
as a man in love not with the notion
of love but with someone in a body
like this one. Stubborn as the woman

perched stiffly on the end of your bed,
whom you mean to convince you know
better than she knows herself.
How can you be sure?

What Dances

I see the way you look at me,
the way you want to touch me.

You flatter yourself. What I want
is something more hopeless.

The red shoes of a girl whose feet
couldn't stay still, who finally

found a man who would cut them off
out of love. The red wedding shoes

of a man whose wife left him shortly
for someone more broken, less kind.

Newman praised a light that seemed
to beckon, calling it kinder

than the dark it cut. I'm not so sure.
I saw a road ignite at the collision

of sleep and death, and only death
rose, radiant, leading me on.

If I say you're beautiful,
which the situation seems to demand,

I mean I love the hand of light
resting on your shoulder, and would

put my hand there, letting it burn
while I gaze past you at what

I really love, into the shadow
beyond us where night deepens and holds.

Going to Sleep

There is no reason why because it is dark you should look at
things differently from when it is light. The hell there isn't!
I figured that all out once, and for six months I never slept with
the electric light off.

—Jake Barnes, in The Sun Also Rises

It's simple.
I turn to the wall and say flatly,
Friend, things are hard all over,
today—today I tripped in the flower bed,
spilling the paint meant for the rocks.

I'll have to repaint the roses.
We want to look our best,
stepping from the red bushes, eyes very bright,
dance slippers in hand, only a little late,
a little red from rehearsal.

And out of practice. Sewn back into
the worn-out costume of forgetfulness.
Hearing footsteps, turning wrong,
spilling the bouquet on the piano, bumping
into the clock ringing 13, 14, 15.

Things are not working.
A nightgown caught on thorns, a shoe
full of weeds stuffed into a pillow.
Who spilled salt in the bed?
Who painted the flowers with soap?

I lie on my back.
I put a handkerchief over one hand.
When I pull the cloth away the hand
is still a hand. Tonight this is magic.
I close my eyes and try again.

The Palace at 4 A.M.

I catch myself sighing.
There is snow in the east wing.
Ice announces itself in the ballroom,

but the guests have gone.
The children's beds are empty,
my sister and I dressed for school,

waiting in the field for the train
that raises the dust on the piano,
that stops a woman in old slippers

who dances alone. Who is she?
Whose yellow hat sails past the window,
the old moon in here on the mantel?

I stop dancing. My feet are cold,
my hands too stiff to play.
Out of the cold, the late hour,

the restlessness, one makes
—what? A rock. A cloud. A blanket.
Furniture for the next act, a duet

with a stranger, a colonel,
instruments tuned after years of disuse,
playing music never rehearsed,

always for the *next* act. Outside,
a train whistle cuts across the dark.
In my uneasy sleep my sister and I

run across the field towards the train.
The new regiment at last?
I get up from the piano

and go to the window. There is no train,
no field under the first snow.

Long-Distance Swimming

From the pale bed in the faint room,
I recapture the colorless water
solid against my mechanical strokes,
the amphibian chill of long immersion.
Who needed air? As if inland,

an island-like house reared up,
dissolved to a block of stores.
Threading through stacked linens,
bolts of cloth, I was chased by a voice, or voices,
or heading into them, who dryly called warmth.

Something I lashed at, someone dragged me
into a rocking chair of a boat,
a sodden man who looked from my ropy arms
to his hands and back to the burns
imprinted where he'd touched me.

Against the window, flowers, like events,
transpire with the casual intimacy
of strangers, the cool proximity
of *casual* to *casualty*. The dead skin
is a strange gift. I feel nineteen again,

daily swimming in a pool too short,
nights selling refreshments in a third-run movie house.
Once two men bumbled into the fluorescence,
one saying, "Five years ago,
that would have been a happy ending."

II

You know that, according to quantum theory, if two particles collide with enough energy you can, in principle, with an infinitesimal probability, produce two grand pianos.

—I. I. Rabi

Grisaille

Given enough fragments, close
enough together, the eye will perceive
a whole—the persistence of vision,

so that at twenty-four frames per second,
a man appears to be walking smoothly
—away from some crime or toward

the assignation with an ordinary woman.
Too familiar with his own aquiline lines,
he finds the broad planes of her peasant's

face foreign, exotic. But is the movie
going to warm up or will he,
in the remaining hour, manage only

to remove her spectacles? You flee
the film's formal garden, burst
into what's left of the day,

into what you'd forgotten,
the bleached, grainy texture of sun
panning over snow. A window winks freshly;

you bear the defenseless look
of that woman without her customary glasses.
Someone is threatening to love you,

thrusting you into the path
of onrushing contentment. No,
not exactly. More transient, a kiss

grazing the juncture of lips and cheek,
this dry snow whistling against you.
The shadow of one flake where it lodges on another.

Sleeping Beauty

Map-makers of old used to call the "terra incognita" blanks
"sleeping beauties."

The first hundred years passed quickly.
She slept, or pretended to sleep,
until no one burst into her chamber
to cry "Your Majesty, the New World,
a conspiracy of cartographers
. . . oh"

There was a land between sleeping and waking
where a sentry forgot everything,
his name, the password, the enemy,
everything but sleep.
He would betray himself but to whom?
She found herself there too.

She tried to go back to sleep.
The friar fell asleep
over the queen mother's confession.
China fell asleep in its silks.
Tired of the endless hunt of the tapestry
where the unicorn never escaped,
she moved to the rose garden.
She practiced until, for her,
there was only a growing cold,
the fall, the frost, the stiffening
under a first kiss,
a beginning of something at last.

Patches of Sky

Like a map blanketing a bed,
the flat fields slope enough so
under snow at sunrise some are coral,
some cornflower—cartographer's tints
taken from an old quilt.

Four hawks revolve over the square
where the wind has hollowed out a house,
and the next one, where it fills a tree
with feathered leaves, beaked cries.
Or so I say. Expansive for once,

I want to show you a countryside,
not a bed. Look—low hills folding
over centuries and at their base
someone's ragged crocuses
in what must have been a garden,

a civilizing introduction of the frivolous
to dirt that supports not much but itself.
Think of the first tenants of this house,
two schoolteacher spinsters.
Did they wear red,

the intensity missing in the view?
What held them, sisters, together?
They slept, one on each side
of the double fireplace, under these quilts.
Look—the dark side of each square

is patched from a man's old suits,
the light from flowered dresses.
Did one of them ever feel like this,
asking who she belonged to,
the other answering, "Whom?"

Trappings

You take his arm, his coat,
his shirt, letting him down

into the fields of your bed. He slips
into sleep, leaving to you,

as to the others, the weighing
of comfort, or fatigue,

against desire. He doesn't
need you as much as rest.

Do you mind? His eyelashes
smudge your shoulder bone.

That boy on the street this evening,
with hands loose and worn

from crime, had the long eyes
of your sister. Of the wings

of the moth pinned up
in your father's study. Where you're stuck

in a stiff-backed chair, measuring
the angle of apology. Memory's

varnished imperfections. The jostling
furniture, the closing room

want everything back,
but you're down, out on the street,

heading, like the boy, for the life
you mean to take.

The Invention of Routine

The last event. The bareback rider
turns smaller and smaller circles
in the dimming spotlight until her horse
is following its own gilded tail.

The others have all ridden off,
packed and slipped out of town
while the sheriff sits, rapt,
in the front row for the third night

and she is left turning,
waiting for the music to stop,
her arms tight on the horse's neck,
the animal's rough breathing against her own,
the worn costume snagging on branches,

until she catches up with the rest of the show
in the next town, the next state,
where she is privately, terribly sure
they've been before.

White Fields

I walk into the thicket
of my family, for a photograph,
thinking, who would find me here?
The snow on the east face
of the hill, in the last light,
burns like a cheek.
The moon, its thinnest, begins
to burn too. I offer it
as small comfort, in my absence.

Another morning without sun.
The geese I heard on waking,
moving from river to wheatfield,
flew above the clouds.
I spend the morning in the attic
looking for something to abandon.
You would laugh at this.
You call again to ask
why I'm not with you.

I tell you how I found a place,
just over the hill that edges this town,
where I was all that stood
between ground and sky. I felt
cloudlike, lying low for a season.

I tell you a dream.
Across the white fields of winter
you come, long shadow,
looking for something in the snow,
a woman in a white dress.
You bring a shirt the color
of sagebrush in spring,
which you've never seen.
Your face is the color of sand.

A bad connection, static
all that's between us.
I think of you as the horizon.
I think of you.

The Painter's Model

The man in the orchard called
for another canvas. Dropping the parasol
he had posed me with, I stretched,
gathered my skirts, and ran to the house,
cursing the changeable world.

How long had he stood me there?
The tree, barely limned in charcoal,
to be filled in later, was filled in.
The whole worm-eaten orchard
went up for sale as firewood. That

was several canvases ago. He blames,
and loves, the inconstant shadows. I think
that when he mutters, "Beautiful!"
in what seems to be my direction,
he does not mean me exactly
but the way, at that instant,

the light glazes my clouds of clothes
or, when I undress, lays
a wash from thigh to belly
to breast. I think he's in love
with the layers of air that wrap us
like the nimbus of a saint.

But something must escape his brush.
Why else, come fall, does he start
a fire of dead leaves, throw in
six paintings, and stand back to let
the flames catch in every shade of ocher?

Fall

This weather calls to mind only
itself, years earlier. Another house
and the night a man climbed
from the upstairs window to a tree
while a party burned out below.
He was never found.

                    A night like this,
on the edge of fall, when cold
is discovered by a single cricket
that sends its message fitfully,
I like to picture the man, slightly drunk,
elated by his discovery that there was
nothing he couldn't leave behind.

Did he drive south into the next day,
stopping only for a quick haircut
before crossing the border?

Did he stop at the bridge and get out
to watch the fingers of mist
trail over the black water?

Did he stay in the tree, swaying,
hugging the trunk, until the first light
spilled out of its bottle? Then what?

I don't mean to suggest
that he was dying any more
than the rest of us. All I know
is that he kept what he had
by leaving it.

The Man on the Bed

In late September 1958, I visited his South Truro studio and
saw on the easel not an unfinished painting, nor even a
stretched canvas, but a large empty stretcher. "He's been look-
ing at that all summer," Jo Hopper said.
                                —Lloyd Goodrich, of Edward Hopper

He lay on the bed, thinking
of what he could see from the window
as a little landscape of failure,
glittering after the rain,
the roses within reach but rusted,
a red bird lost in the thick
wet leaves of the oak,
the tree, caught in mirrors, shaking.
He lay on the bed,
his shirt turning blue with evening,
thinking, in the dark a red bird
might as well be black.

He slept then
and dreamt of a man
who slept with his glasses on,
the easier to find them when he woke.
The room seemed smaller,
the wind against the corner
of the house stronger.
If the heart is a house, he thought,
it is rented to strangers
who leave it empty.
If the heart is a house,
it is also the darkness around it
through which a black bird flies, unseen,
and unseeing, into the window,
beating and beating its wings
against the glass.

34

Not You

I wanted to be the man with two pairs of shoes,
the day brown or black.
I wanted to be the cook in the all-night diner
cutting onions, rubbing his eyes.
I wanted to be the man at the corner waiting
at three A.M. for the light to change,
for five A.M. and dawn, something
to send him home.

The window is cool and hard against my cheek.
In your chair I shift and the wood creaks;
it means nothing in the way
the old and familiar mean nothing.
Or nothing right.
                            The dream of a house
almost like this one. The rooms shift,
I slip on the watery floor, there is a man
at the kitchen table who isn't you.

I want to be you, your sleep
unreached by the birds outside
calling for light.
I want to be you, your measured breathing.

To Make You Well

I wanted to be the miller's daughter,
spinning straw into gold,
gold into straw, indifferently.

At night I lie beside you
in the rough, shy underclothes
that are always left
no matter how far you undress me.

Tonight my hand,
raw as if from spinning,
is cool on your forehead.
In your fever, you brush away the wings.
I see again the crows
that circled above the field today,
never coming down.

A scarecrow. In the dark
I run my hand along your shoulder—
the bony points are sharper than ever.
Another month's blood lost
between us. This
is as close as I can come.
I have no magic. You must sleep.

Sea Change

Minus tide. In an old coat but barefoot,
I trailed across sand flats
into a luminous fog. What wet light—
a thick glow that failed to illuminate,

a clarity so circumscribed I thought
of old theories: the earth a dish
balanced on a dozen columns
or the back of a turtle. What use

were such notions? Held in the right light,
they could have reflected the holder,
like the dream you had after your wife's
sudden death—that she had instead

taken a lover. You seemed to take
some comfort in this change of pains,
said you preferred it to the dream
of walking this stretch, feet stung with cold,

lungs damp, and following in mind's eye
someone whose familiar gait swiftly
outdistanced your memory.
The world does have edges beyond which

the dead lie, in another element,
like the deep fish that, dragged to the surface,
explode. Even sea salt, its sweaty,
womanly pungency could conjure

nothing sympathetic. *Memento mori*,
that's what it becomes, rime of decay
on the water's detritus. Shallow bowls
of sand have caught the offerings:

little crab under a chipped whelk, half
a ragged scallop shell, bottleneck crusted
with limpets, shard of a bisque doll's face
abraded until featureless.

Closing

I take down the window
and the hill behind it,
the lake just over the hill,
the moon risen over the lake.

And you, prepared for this entrance
since the show opened,
set out across the ice
looking for a wife in the corn fields.

My hair catches in the door as you leave.
Well, cut it off. Quick, more rope.
I push the last elephant
into the truck with a promise:

tomorrow in a pasture anywhere
he'll be painted white,
a target on the heart, fair game.
I start a note,

"Nothing to wear but fear.
I have a dream that I'm flying.
My feathers fall out
into the hands of a stranger. Yours."

III

If the sky falls they shall have clouds for supper.
—Charles Simic

Night Freight

Even absence is not as separate
as sleep. Consider the man
who liked to wake at this hour
to think of a woman he'd left
in another city; then, he said,
he could imagine her; then
she was doing nothing.

Four A.M. Leaves of the nut trees
rattle above the drone of night freight
a mile or more away, the sound borne
over the valley as over water.
On this island of a little light,
like an early archaeologist
uncovering a *kouros*, I puzzle
your solid rest, that archaic smile.

When, in sleep, you turn to me,
I could be any woman, just bones
of contention. A librarian
confronted by what pictures
can't reveal—rapt composure
of a Gothic saint, rigid repose
of a mere knight, the stone stretched
on a sarcophagus—I'm weighing sleep

against the conception of it:
a third of your life prone, parallel
to the ground, as if in rehearsal.
This must be the librarian's nightmare:
always new entries in the catalogue
of the missing. And somewhere
the untaken measure of a difficult
calendar for one of us, alone.

Calibrations

Some movements, like the clock's,
can't really be calibrated: pointless
to stare at the hands when you should sleep.
It's simply *a while* before you can identify
the scrap of light blinking through the room,
throwing angles fitfully into relief—
a firefly knocking the eaves for a way out
now that it's bumbled in, refugee
from smudge pots tufting a woolen dark.

They're to blanket the blooming orchard,
as if it were some delicate kid,
with smoke against unseasonable cold.
Wrapped for the first watch,
your old friend's daughter looked
like his sturdy sisters, not the sapling
you were used to. So a girl's body
takes on the measure of a woman's;
her mind learns to work like her father's.
And you see in her something she can't remember.

Winking a red eye then a green, a small plane
crawls up the sky. After the old man
takes his turn, you're to busy yourself
nursing the little fires and not
stand stamping, whistling into your hands,
watching for the mercury's last drop.
Or a welcome sun to relieve you.
Stumbling up to the house at dawn,
you'll come upon the night's kill,
winged creatures that didn't weather.

44

You'll fall on the couch, not even
removing your boots, not wanting bed
but to be wakened by father and daughter
rising again to their different chores.

Myopia

Given the hour, the sea
has ridden up to the house,
touched, and slipped back,
navigating the dark

as if it were natural. It is.
It isn't. Closing my eyes,
I hear my mother laugh
over the miles. And what else?

The blurred world draws us
out of ourselves, the water here
tonight inverting her sand.
Against a displaced sun,

against a lunar porch light,
some nocturnal bird may be
just a scrap of paper
in a wind. The hand leading

this page to my weak eye
may not be mine. The figure
across the water could be a post,
or a stump, or if it moves,

a friend. I put on my glasses.
There is, rising, the moon
that surprised my grandfather
with its sharp edges.

Pulled by the earth,
it blindly pulls back.

You try thinking of the headache as a hat,
its broad brim skimming the water,
and then, where the straw is cracked,
the crown filling until just the tip
of a ratty feather sails. You know the wing,
you realize, from the secondhand costumes
of a woman you lived with.

The water is being painted
by an amateur who, as you watch,
muddies it, working too fast, too expressly
for the benefit of an audience. He's ignored
by the kid towing a newspaper kite
and by a swan, strayed from the city park,
circling like a loose boat. *Under*,

the waves rumble to the gravel, *under*,
under. That's what you'll have her hear
when you write about leaving her
for a larger-breasted woman
with better education. You'll say you were
married and add a child, all the trappings.

In the landlocked town where the story's set,
your "wife" will miss the shabby ocean,
a fact your readers will take as symbolic.
They may pity her but will understand
that your insomnia is caused by more
than oppressive summer weather.

They won't guess her unsimplified side of it,
the boxes she wouldn't unpack or throw out,
her stern refusal to say why she smiled.
There's a secret to this but it's not yours.
From what the ocean throws back
someone could try to compose a catalogue
of what it's saving.

Any Story

They were very lady-writer stories. . . . The kind of stories where the man puts down his fork and the woman knows it's all over.

—Lillian Hellman

Make it any story you like.
She rebuttoned her blouse, surprised
that her fingers knew what to do,

and pinned up her hair. The sea,
shot with silver, tilted toward her
and then away, and her white shirt glowed

in the porch's deep air. She watched
the wind beat the wild roses colorless
on the sea wall, then move its hands

over the long body of a girl
who climbed out of the water
to find her skin chased with gold, hard

in the sun's bath. The wind rattled
the china, and she turned back to the man
whose hands knew the dumb mysteries

of fear and said, "Your tea has cooled."
Those were my mother's words as she,
in a dress of beads and breezes,

turned to the child who, in the presence
of such an apparition, knew herself
to be plainer than the brown liquid

in the flowered cup that this beautiful,
half-familiar stranger had offered her,
a taste like a glimpse at a keyhole

of a room that turned out to be dark.
It was any story you like.
It was—it was anything but this.

After Iceland, William Morris Dreams of Panama

This color, outside all theory,
insists only on fact:
there are a hundred thousand greens,

each one truer than the last, and blue,
more sky than I have ever seen.
Clothes are blinding white,

the only choice if one is not to melt.
The second day I trade my paint box
for dark glasses and tinted postcards

in a language I have yet to understand.
And come home to England tamed,
straw hat in hand, a parrot on a chain,

the white suit worn gray,
not nearly warm enough,
and am not recognized by anyone.

Business

Off the shallow stage, it is my business
to see that your collar is fastened,
yours, on the set, to worry the starched cloth
until its corners snap loose. Rakish,

you tilt an excuse for a chair
as the audience begins to suspect
you're doomed. This is your favorite part,
the one that kills you, that after this act

you walk away from. When the stagehand
fires the blanks, you're usually outside,
painted face absurdly sculptural
in the alley's more natural light.

Over the intercom, I can hear the actress
whose role is to love you hurling herself
into that chair, which doesn't survive.
Is that funny? Tonight's audience

sounds unsure the furniture wasn't valuable.
What do they know? The closed rooms
in which scenes are unplotted and unrehearsed,
scenes you will have to imagine or imitate.

You know how they begin—out of habit
a man rises from bed and raises his voice
to be heard over an intimate din
for the first of how many times this day.

The bay gone solid overnight
will not budge in the sun's
oblique chill. This is the dead
of winter, the fisherman dragged in,
frozen, from a scalloper's nets.

Old grudges lodge in the heart's
warmest room; the old lady below us
sleeps to her radio squalling.
What can we do? Fall on each other
out of boredom, or desperation,

in the name of something else?
I stare out the window. I am always
staring out the window. There was a girl
who spent days like this, nights on ice,
skating towards a ghost ship, lit

with a happiness the world took
for an idiot's beatific grin.
You look up from a letter to a woman
who admires the slant of your mind,
the angles of your lean body

as you bend into listening.
She has offered, or has yet to ask,
to sleep with you. A friendly gesture?
What can be made light of
is made light of. What must be harbored

sets sail for spring and freezes.

Natural Forces

Take the specific
gravity of certain matters,
the lopsided attractions that can
loop things into opposite quarters.

So that, on two coasts, we end
another day upright, throwing out
the long shadows of the discrete.
So that, the earth curving

in its slow whirl under rust-voiced birds,
today began sooner here. Picture it:
a town on sand borrowed from water.
The physical bond of bay

and moon. The weathering
of board and beach. The bed
that a man, whose face you can't
make from the grayed light,

leans over, bent on taking your daughter
out of some dream she shudders in.
Intent on proving her happy
to that wretched judge, herself.

Bad judge of distance
and its unfaithful lover, now
held in the attractive net
of this relative stranger, I lie

still, fixed in the grid
of constancy, the contours of loss
at once familiar. A kiss comes close
but the draw of earth goes deeper,

down to what will not give.

The Life of the Remittance Man

. . . in colonial parlance, a Ne'er-do-well living in the colonies on quarterly remittances received from friends "at home."
                                                              —E. B. Hodge

What do you think it's like?
A lonely man in a big garden
trying his hand at painting one
of the beautiful women around him?
Suggesting that she remove her blouse?

No mail. The check is late again.
No sulky chambermaid to tease
about a message in the mirror's dust.
No message. Nothing not covered
with a rubbed, gray velvet.

The color of an old smoking jacket
that would, were it not so worn,
remind one of something else.
A well-kept lawn, perhaps, where,
like a spotless handkerchief

in a breast pocket, a table is set for tea.
One cup. One bowl and spoon. The articles
of a small faith. Today hot water seems
miraculous. Or take the bed's
standing invitation to the horizontal,

which a cloud accepts as I'm considering it.
A man who paints with black
wears it too. A man who can't live
with himself lives alone, in a dry country,
where even color is fugitive.

Take the patch of sky at the one window.
I praise its dullness and my own.
Some days here one could be blinded
by a blank sheet of paper.

Knowing

that in sleep your body fits
the curve of mine. No,
that I start from sleep,

from dreaming my body blue,
the heart stiff, to you, your head
on my numbed shoulder. So, I am here

in ordinary geography.
The rain of pine needles
continues on the roof, a whispering

I can't make out. That your edges
lie somewhere beyond me. The house
shudders, or you do in the cold,

the dream of cold. It occurs to me
that what sounds like the sea is,
given our location, the sea.

My father hearing the whistling
wings of migrating cranes
before he could see them

is somewhere else. Did he know
what I am unlearning now?
Against will, without design,

my body has been making
concessions, skin knowing
what the mind can only guess.

Crossing the Plains

I'm in a most peculiar frame of mind tonight. I want like the
devil to live.
—Vershinin, in *Three Sisters*

Halfway home,
at a place unmarked on the map,
he stops.
He has never seen a place this flat
and is filled with a terrible happiness, vast and empty.

He opens the trunk, throws open suitcases,
fills the air with birds
and hundreds of handkerchiefs.
A forest of chairs springs up,
empty.

He stands still for so long
a thin frost begins to glisten
like little mirrors on his cold coat.
And who is reflected there?
He feels transparent.

This part of the trip he will never speak of—
the emptiness a lightness,
a movable island of joy,
a reason to go on.

A Second or Third Dimension

In stealth, snow inhabits the sky
cleanly, and in the laundry room
a short, old woman folds a bed sheet
by herself without its brushing the floor.

She's detail in a faded tapestry,
maybe the cloth used, after a peasant revolt,
to protect a cellar of potatoes
from freezing. As foreground,

juncos shake flakes from their beaks,
scrounging a seedy meal. Like *mille fleurs*,
the snow fills in, dendrites
and hexagonal plates; and the sky's a solid

that dancers and pilots would recognize.
A spinning of snow. A skin,
like the skins of paper you spoke of,
as you erased part of a drawing, leaving

only the suggestion of a figure,
or perhaps two, a bed risen from
and left unmade, or a shirt slung over the back
of a chair. Each succeeding surface

responded more crudely, less accommodating
to your careful strokes. What
does this intimate, friend? There may be
lives under this one, remote and eroded lives.

Bearings

I am going to school myself so well in things that, when I try
to explain my problems, I shall speak, not of self, but of
geography.

—Pablo Neruda

Caught on the shoals of an afternoon,
the bags I emptied to make room for salt
fill with sand.

Long ago this morning
there was a room and I was in it.
Some things were probable—
corners, the right angle
of body to floor, loss of wings,
the invention of absence,
a gap I couldn't see
where the wind blew and made no sound—
where I am now,

where this evening you come in
just ahead of the dark.
Difficulty, I have to love you
for myself. It is not too late.
Tomorrow we can put the ocean
behind us and move inland
toward the open country of the heart,
the worst already imagined,
one step ahead of ourselves.

Field Glass

Bleached grass, in the wind,
makes the motions of water
up waves of hills. You have claimed
there's a chapel in Vence where,
surrounded by yellows, blues, and greens,
a visitor doesn't note the absence of red
so much as supply what's missing.

I'm not about to argue, watching you
tilt your head back to drain the last
of your drink, your dark glasses blankly
reflecting the sky. Handfuls of clouds
are blowing over, decorative promises
of nothing. A hundred years ago,
two women tied on red skirts,
that they might be easily seen,
roped themselves together, and clambered
genteelly up a small mountain.

In the lot next door a twist of dust
spins itself out. The spindly tree
shudders at a ghost of breeze
we didn't catch, damp islands
spreading on your shirt. This season
a drop of water equals a magnifying lens,
so you irrigate by night
that your gardens won't burn.

Last night, waked from sweaty sleep
by something you couldn't identify,
not recognizing the room's
dark-rounded angles, you mistook
the wet patter outside for rain.
And another part of the country
where, on a day as clear as this,
blue stretched along the horizon
would not be more sage-covered hills
but the sea—in the distance, another solid.

Hard Water

Late, late yestreen I saw the new moone,
  Wi' the auld moone in hir arme,
And I feir, I feir, my deir master,
  That we will cum to harme.
                              —"Sir Patrick Spens"

What are the treasures of darkness? Tonight
neither the moon nor the man who would be walking
home in its watery light but for one thing.

Where is he? Trees spread their nets
over dry houses. What slips through? A school
of clouds that will tear at the moon's hook.

Under a bridge a man wraps in the sail
of the cold, as a hermit crab fits its fragile body
into a shell's spiral, into the grit and roar

of such rest. Why doesn't he move
as spindrift mist washes over him? Does he dream
he's small craft in a wine sea? Does he sleep?

A tree too light for the wind's waves
loses its mast. The body of the man
under the bridge is too heavy for the moon's tug.

Flat-bottomed cloud, soft ferry,
bear him over this saltwater-blurred city.
Bear him home.

Library of Congress Cataloging in Publication Data

Greger, Debora, 1949-
 Movable islands.
 (Princeton series of contemporary poets)
 I. Title.
PS3557.R42M68   811'.5'4   79-3212
ISBN 0-691-06422-9
ISBN 0-691-01369-1 pbk.